Puff the Pup

Written by Tony Mitton
Illustrated by James Cottell

Collins

Puff the pup dug a pit.

A lot was in it.

But it was just a pot.

But a frog was in the pot.

But the frog did not stop.

It hopped to the pond.

Story map

Ideas for reading

Written by Clare Dowdall, PhD
Lecturer and Primary Literacy Consultant

Reading objectives:
- use phonic knowledge to decode regular words and read them aloud accurately
- read and understand simple sentences
- demonstrate understanding when talking with others about what they have read

Communication and language objectives:
- answer "how" questions about their experiences and in response to stories or events
- listen to stories, accurately anticipating key events and respond to what they hear with relevant comments, questions or actions
- express themselves effectively, showing awareness of listeners' needs

Curriculum links: Knowledge and Understanding of the World; Creative Development

Focus phonemes: u, ff, g, o, f, r, h

Fast words: the, was

Word count: 67

Build a context for reading

- Discuss what children know about puppies, e.g. who has had one; how do they behave?
- Revise the focus phoneme *ff*. Ask children to suggest words that contain this phoneme and model writing them, e.g. puff, huff, stuff.
- Read the title together. Add sound buttons and practise blending the sounds to read *Puff the Pup*.
- Read the blurb on the back cover together. Model blending sounds and rereading for fluency. Ask children to discuss what they think will happen in the story.

Understand and apply reading strategies

- Walk through the book together, looking at the pictures and discussing the events. Dwell on p7 and model how to read the longer word *d-u-m-p*.
- Ask children to read the book aloud from the beginning to the end, sounding out and blending to read the words.
- Move around the group, listening to them blending through words independently, praising their blending and fluent reading.
- Invite fast finishers to share the book with a partner, finding their favourite part in the story.